Praise for *I'm Alwa*

"Karisma Price speaks with a wink, a sigh, a kni   's so
serious. She speaks as someone raised on a gumbo of James Baldwin and j̶a̶̶ oker,
buckjumping and Brooklyn. She speaks as your phone's autocorrect, your remixed
song lyrics, your friendly neighborhood fortune-teller. Price speaks directly to and for
you while speaking distinctly for herself. These are the masterful portraits, mercurial
testimonies, and verbal inventions of our imminent poet of the new school/south, the
next generation. *I'm Always so Serious* is brilliant."

—Terrance Hayes, winner of the National Book Award for *Lighthead*

"In *I'm Always so Serious*, Karisma Price takes an unflinching look at personal, familial,
racial, historical, and national violences in order to celebrate her survival of them. But
Price is honest about the cost of that survival: 'I refuse to make either of us cry in
this poem so // I'll just tell you that the willow weeps.' These poems are intimate in
ways that enlist our inclusion as readers in every line and scene. And yet, they are bold
enough to mark and make clear a city as romantic and mythologized as New Orleans.
This is a brilliant debut by a poet we should continue to watch."

—Jericho Brown, winner of the Pulitzer Prize for *The Tradition*

"*I'm Always so Serious* is, naturally, bursting with humor. It laughs in the dark. It plays
in the cemetery. In this stunning first collection, Karisma Price has crafted a voice that's
blunt and sharply observant, witty but earnest, and excitingly flexible. Whether lyrical,
formal, or experimental, these poems approach language masterfully, with intimacy
and adventure. Wry and introspective with painterly description and enormous heart,
this book absolutely shines. It flaunts its black aliveness and revels while in anguish. It's
the tender part in conversation with the hard edge."

—Morgan Parker, winner of the National Book Critics Circle Award
for *Magical Negro*

"'Each of my days is a failed manifesto,' Price writes in this fearless, bristling debut,
and happily for us, this falling short of declaring herself conclusively means that her
days yield poems instead of platforms—lyrics alive with striving and open to discovery,
full of idiosyncrasy, insight, and surprise. This isn't to say that where the poet stands
(politically and otherwise) is ever anything less than clear as day, but what she finds

there is existence in all its telescoping complexity—the public sphere, the intimate; the minute detail and enormous truths; history's voices still audible in the present; and above all, the saving grace of music and life's 'little sugars shining' amid the pain of loss, loneliness, and injustice. As formally inventive as it is fully inhabited, *I'm Always so Serious* does what a first book should—it introduces us to a voice at once new and familiar, satisfies us deeply, and leaves us aching to hear what more the poet has to tell and eager to see how she tells it."

—Timothy Donnelly, winner of the Kingsley Tufts Poetry Award
for *The Cloud Corporation*

"In her vital debut *I'm Always so Serious*, Karisma Price assembles a choir. On the first page, Oppen duets with André 3000. Later, Homer and Baldwin croon. Throughout the collection, Price's casts dazzle—Douglas Kearney, Ella Fitzgerald, Cher, Gwendolyn Brooks, Frank Ocean, and Ringo Starr all make important appearances. Price summons these titans to harmonize with her own singular and unforgettable voice, rendering a blooming bouquet of lyric moments I will never forget—lines like, 'There is ample. / Ample is here.' Like, 'My father was a soft violence taken by a softer violence.' Like, 'Baby, I have broken / the trees for you.' I'm getting goosebumps just typing them now. These poems are better than good; they're undeniable."

—Kaveh Akbar, author of *Pilgrim Bell*

"This book is the radiant debut of a true blues poet. Stitching together everyday objects, cherished wreckage, and embodied memories, Karisma Price doesn't have to raise her voice higher than a rich hum for us to hear the howl seething under every line in *I'm Always so Serious*. Be warned, though: in the precise and devastating moments that she does decide to unleash that unbridled rage, you will have no choice but to join her howl."

—Saeed Jones, author of *Prelude to Bruise*

"Karisma Price's poems are detail rich like a memoir that always exceeds comfort by letting things have their own true size and fact and if these deft poems were a government (and we lived 'under' it) we would be the lucky citizens of the only wild and just place on the planet."

—Eileen Myles, author of *For Now*

"The poems in *I'm Always so Serious* shimmer with formal dexterity, brim with literary innovation, and sing a new song of the South. There were times reading this book when I would finish a poem, look around, and audibly say 'How did she just do that?' Karisma Price is an astonishing writer, and this book is a fantastic debut."
—Clint Smith, winner of the National Book Critics Circle Award for *How the Word Is Passed: A Reckoning with the History of Slavery Across America*

"There are poetry collections and then there are *poetry collections*. *I'm Always so Serious*, Karisma Price's striking debut, is the latter. If you're a poet, you'll wish you would've written 'God / watches me through a viewfinder whispering, / *It'll be worse next time. It'll be your mother.*' If you're a reader, you'll wonder, 'How did she know "we are as lonely as every room / without a piano"?' I'm both a writer and reader of poems, and so am doubly floored. Price has written one hell of a first book."
—Nicole Sealey, author of *Ordinary Beast*

"Karisma Price has given us a phenomenal collection—inventive, exhilarating, and crackling with honesty—that is deeply worth our time and attention. But the real magic of *I'm Always so Serious* is its exquisite balance of tough questions with gorgeous pockets of hope. A breathtaking debut."
—Jami Attenberg, *New York Times* bestselling author of *The Middlesteins*

"A book that navigates several locales and mythologies: Greek, New Orleans, and New York. Karisma Price is a technician of the intimate and the nuanced. She depicts the streets with as much genius as she revels within the fractured realm of the remembered. Poetry lovers should rejoice at the breathtaking inventiveness to be found on each page. *I'm Always so Serious* heralds the arrival of a brilliant voice that has come to dissect, reinterpret, and clarify. And this book will be dissected and paid homage to. *I'm Always so Serious* is a book of poetry that begs to be reread after the last page is turned. Gift *I'm Always so Serious* to your friends. They will thank you."
—Maurice Carlos Ruffin, author of *The Ones Who Don't Say They Love You*

"Karisma Price's *I'm Always so Serious* is an absolute force. With language so deftly selected, it's a book where the self maintains its place gloriously at the center of the story, always insisting on its truth as its heartbeat drives the poem. Abundant with graceful language that speaks to life's joys and sufferings, *I'm Always so Serious* tells the tale of a self that has lifted itself into a new sort of existence—one where poetry is within the heart of everything. The book resounds, 'I wanted to hold your voice / to my ear like a secret.' You will find yourself holding the music of these poems to your ear like a prayer. I love this book and this poet, and you will, too."

—Dorothea Lasky, author of *Animal*

"Karisma Price has written the book I've needed at every stage of my life. *I'm Always so Serious* brought me home and lifted me to those Black southern abundant places that raised and razed me. Rarely, if ever, do we get this much stylized wonder in one singular book. It's incredible."

—Kiese Laymon, author of *Heavy: An American Memoir*

"How does one begin to speak about poems that continue to speak, that continue to challenge, so long after the page is turned? *I'm Always so Serious* is a book of immense teachings—a stunning, tender debut that gathers us (in the Black sense) by the ear. Poems that can't help but signify. They peer out from one vantage point and escape into another. Even now, I hear them ringing in my neighbor's throat. This is the power of Karisma's Black Southern poetics, and her rendering of adolescence where we learn so early that 'everything around us / is measured in blood.' This book shows us what language can do, how it leaps in and against our favor. That's no easy task, a testimony fueled by introspection where even the poet isn't off the hook. This is what I mean by haunting work. We already know the facts. Karisma gives us the truth of the matter."

—Malcolm Tariq, author of *Heed the Hollow*

"In the opening pages of *I'm Always so Serious*, chairs appear frequently, which may be a subtle way of suggesting you ought to be sitting down as you read these wholly original poems that will undo you as you enter Karisma Price's acts of witness, love, protest, tenderness. The world of these poems is both familiar and strange, a world where domestic details take on the numinous, harrowing truth of her compassionate witness. Reading Price, who in one poem braids Baldwin and Homer together, you might recall Baldwin's words about empathy, a quality that pulses through these poems: 'It was books that taught me that the things that tormented me most were the very things that connected me with all the people who were alive or who had ever been alive.' I am glad to be alive in the same space-time as Price, who is guide, companion, emcee, absence, love, pure audacity rowing us through Katrina's floodwaters, through 'the blue suede of the casket,' 'the *clack clack* of movement,' and the rest of America, asking, 'In what way would *you* like to be devastated?'"

—Catherine Barnett, author of *Human Hours*

"*I'm Always so Serious* honors its name with enduring elegies; love songs for the vulnerable; and fantastically formal verses that pinpoint what aches after the water has resolved its hunger, who bucks to the sound of their own clarion. Here, 'History almost unchained itself // from my weaker clavicle. / Everyone looked,' and instead of shying away, these poems navigate through an odyssey of its own making: Black, tragic, and lit up from the inside with the possibility of family. 'I tell you I want to exist / without interference,' she writes, and who are we to interfere with such an impressive debut?"

—Phillip B. Williams, author of *Thief in the Interior*

"Karisma Price's poems unfold—like hands lifted in praise, like a sharpened pocketknife—into expansive litanies that catalog and exalt Black life amidst so much loss. Everything I love, Price writes, stands with death. The exquisite self-portraits rendered here are shaded and contoured in relation to cherished communities of the dead and to the operations of white supremacy that have wrought such devastation: 'I exist with white / and static stars bursting in the center of my vision.' This remarkable volume expands and contracts across home and displacement, across broken levees and Brooklyn sidewalks, across historical and surreal temporalities, charting the pulse of an American story 'so dark you have no other option but to call it / precious.'"

—Deborah Paredez, author of *Year of the Dog*

"These poems demand you roll up your sleeves and get to work as Price's labor of love and love of craft is felt on every page. Any labor done well creates ease, and that's what these poems do—they are a warm invitation to love ourselves and each other more fiercely, as we address our collective and historical failures. Written from 'a body who loves the mercy of movement,' this is a necessarily serious undoing."

—Marwa Helal, author of *Ante body*

I'M ALWAYS

SO SERIOUS

poems KARISMA PRICE

SARABANDE BOOKS
LOUISVILLE, KY

Publisher's Cataloging-in-Publication Data
(Cassidy Cataloguing Services, Inc.)

Names: Price, Karisma, author.
Title: I'm always so serious : poems / Karisma Price.
Description: Louisville, KY : Sarabande Books, [2023] | Includes bibliographical references.
Identifiers: ISBN: 978-1-956046-04-5 (paperback) | 978-1-956046-05-2 (ebook)
Subjects: LCSH: Black people--Race identity--Poetry. | Families--Poetry. | Loss (Psychology)--
Poetry. | American poetry--African American authors. | LCGFT: Poetry.
Classification: LCC: PS3616.R5267 I4 2023 | DDC: 811/.6--dc23

Cover and interior design by Danika Isdahl
Cover art:
Delita Martin "The Girl Inside"
Gelatin Printing, Conte, Relief, Hand-Stitching, Decorative Papers, Acrylic
47w x 63h
2016
Generously provided by Delita Martin and Black Box Press Studio.

Printed in the USA.
This book is printed on recycled, acid-free paper.

Sarabande Books is a nonprofit literary organization.

This project is supported in part by an award from the National Endowment for the Arts. The
Kentucky Arts Council, the state arts agency, supports Sarabande Books with state tax dollars and
federal funding from the National Endowment for the Arts.

For the ones that raised me:

my parents and New Orleans

CONTENTS

III.

I'm Always so Serious

There will be no other words in the world
But those our children speak.
>   George Oppen,
>   "Sara in Her Father's Arms,"
>   The Materials, 1962

Da Souf got sum to say.
>   André 3000,
>   The Source Awards, 1995

SELF-PORTRAIT

after Chen Chen

As happiness, As the wailing tambourine
that replaced my uncle's gun, As the dancing
it does when he waves it at the man who cut him
off, As the rattle of pills in my father's
hands to slow the multiplying cells,
As me thinking something can be
holy, As a pig, As a poem that doesn't mention
the word *father* or *water* or *drowned*,
As a lie as red as a crow's mouth,
As a streetlight whose bulb never breaks,
As a mother who has a child who's allowed to be
nothing more than their age, As weeknight curfew,
As reparations, As a new car, As a down payment,
As the bay leaf inside the pot of red beans boiling
on Mardi Gras day, As a Zulu coconut, As something
so dark you have no other option but to call it
precious, As a sibling, As a rotten tooth,
As an aunt who has warmed the leftovers
of our family before sundown, As whatever's
left of my skeleton after the family pet
has sucked the sorrow from every bit of my marrow.

I.

I'M ALWAYS SO SERIOUS

which is to say in the winters I dream
of owning a multifloored mansion
in New Orleans. Specifically, one
on St. Charles Ave. with a wraparound
porch and white pillars that would only
see the likes of me if I were
the maid, the midwife, the family
mechanic, Archie Manning,
the maintenance worker,
or the mailman trusted
enough to know the gate's nine
digit passcode and leave
the mail resting on the family's
rain-weathered mahogany
rocking chair. In this particular

dream, I'm the mailman. The marigolds'
red tongues lick the legs
of the chair as I leave
the mail on one of its non-refurbished,
lead-painted arms. Their green
necks rapidly invade the eggshell
painted porch like any poor
soldier in need
of his salt. I rip one
from the ground for the sake
of killing, look it in its yellow
center, a vibrant blister,
before I rub it between
my knuckles and render it
a freshly ground thing.

Looking back, this poem
was only supposed to
be about my sinuses,
how, even in my dreams,
I sneeze at the sight
of untended weeds, flowers
whose mouths unfold
under the brazen light
of the sun. The nightmare
is supposed to be my
allergies, how they only allow
me to love what blooms
from a distance, but in every
dream those vibrant marigolds
keep growing. Their vines
are needle-thin
tumors that keep stretching
crazily onto the porch,
keep making the rocking chair
nervous at its own home.
When I see that rocking chair,
I see blood. It rocks like a heart-
beat running from whatever
is inside that mansion,
or behind it with a whip.

THINGS THAT FOLD
after Jamaal May

My father's voice after the cancer
has spread. A flip phone. A flag.

George Bush's hands, as he pauses
his vacation briefly for thoughts and prayers.

My body next to the potted plant
after my father throws the wooden chair.

A cheaply made chair. A small stack
of clothes. A birthday card.

Milvirtha Hendricks under the American
flag 2 days after Hurricane Katrina.

Her face from the crease
made in her

obituary photo as we use
the newspaper to eat crawfish.

The wrinkles in her forehead.
Floodwater passing

through a broken levee.
My uncle's hands

retaping the attic windows
after the floodwater rises.

My cousins sleeping
in the attic because

no neighbor has a rescue boat.
Black people in distress.

They lay prostrate and call it
prayer. The blankets on my cousins'

shoulders days later, when rescued.
The National Guard's smile as he carries

the neighbor's dog from the flooded
living room. The dog's body around

his neck,
an upside-down flag.

THE MONTH BEFORE YOUR FATHER GOES TO PRISON

you buy the cap gun with the orange tip, your friend
        buys the plastic ammo red as fire ants, and you share
the attention, the middle of the street whose potholes still carry

        contaminated dirt. The rest of America still calls you
a refugee. You wait until a car passes and push the cap gun to the other's
        head like an impatient mother pushing food to her child.

You mean no harm, only to scare the passing cars, hoping to get them to crash
        into a fire hydrant and turn this summer into *Do the Right Thing*.
The cars only honk their horns, make you jump

        on the sidewalk and leave a dent in the neighbor's grass.
Later you spray-paint the gun black, hoping the darkness will make
        anyone surrender to you, you golden child.

Your father is concerned. He says the word *robbery* and you don't
        know if he's asking or telling you. *Will this affect you?*
He is asking the way he asked if you were okay with him selling

        your Game Boy without you knowing. Three weeks into the school year,
he is taken from the house in flip-flops, feet scaly, the leg with the three screws
        pushed inside dragging behind the other, a wounded alligator.

You pray for another flood, something to strip the house and leave you stranded
        the way Lent bulldozes its way into your city and strips
the beads from the necks of drunk tourists.

C. J. PEETE, MAGNOLIA 2004

for Ms. Cheryldale V. Washington

Bless the children who are compared to the white ones. Praise the project bricks and the men inside selling white ones. I know Rodney wanted to be a chemist, but they said fuck that and didn't let him graduate. Bless our rivals in the *Cal-E-O*, the unloved children inside its walls and Calliope for allowing us to butcher her name. Bless every accent that flies out of a child's mouth. God bless the child that's got his own.

Bless every child whose favorite flavor is red and pays 25 cents for the crimson ice that stains the tongue. The syrup oozes down the lips of a toddler who has just learned to curse. We make the Magnolia bloom. *A church is a church but it's not a church unless the people is in it.* We are midnight children inside its walls, the black ink they cannot wipe away. Bless the children raising their mothers' children and every child who has felt the bite of a belt. Praise the child who does not cry when getting beat in front of their friends: *See, you have the courage to get cocky. It won't go through, baby. It won't happen! I don't know of any dumpster in the Magnolia that hasn't been turned into a casket. Do you know how many bodies have been thrown away?*

PRELUDE TO SEPARATION

for my grandmother and her many names:
Boo Boo, Bootsy, Helen Valentine Robinson (1924–2005)

This is the type of weather
we lose matriarchs to but don't
yet know. We will unfurl
the rollers from her hair when we find her,
stroke the blue suede of the casket
before she is lowered into
the brownest part of the earth.
There will be no headstone.
There will be nowhere to sing.
There is something vulgar
in our freedom: months later when we
escape the city and storm
to Mississippi, we cannot bring her.
God does not slap the ground.
The audacity. He won't break it open.

WHAT'S IT LIKE ESCAPING SOMETHING TRYING TO KILL YOU?

A minister blames this on *the slaughter of unborn children*. We enter a tunnel, and my breath holds itself for comfort. My father suggests we find a copy of *The Green Book* and pray over it. A car full of black people driving past Confederate statues. A strawberry zooms past my left ear. The wind smashes it against the bark of cedar. A fish drowns itself in the Mississippi. The one-eyed tabby is not allowed in the hotel. She too will float, but in a different city. Three Ritz crackers on a paper plate. There was a bush separating the hotel from a supermarket. The president tries to separate himself from responsibility, but we see him too. *Put those back. You're not wearing hand-me-down underwear.* I eat lifted grapes. You call it stealing, adults call it building credit. Don't you know I don't know where we are? What to do in a country that never wanted me here? Did you hear the one about God? I am blamed for laughing the hotel room into an awkward silence. My aunt sleeps, deaf as hands in the dark. Two hurricanes in the same week? Such sororal horror.

JESUS IS SO QUIET

on Chef Menteur Highway as the wine bottle
conks the back of her head. The Walmart sign
flashes us, the darkness so black, I can only

see the white of her teeth as she shrieks. I signal
to the police, hoping they will see me summoning
from the rear window. The tin foil covering

Jesus's leftovers tears and the mashed potatoes
spill on the backseat. Collard greens stain
my jeans. The blue and red sirens pull

our car over and the tires' halt stops
our faceless father from striking again.
I am ready to break the scent with my teeth.

I breathe out nothing but *The gas light
cut on. I thought we'd crash*, in the voice
of the child I am who wants nothing

but a family to continue living in the type
of quiet a fracture can give to the throat.
The officer pats my shoulder, turns his mouth

up in a watermelon grin. On the ride home,
I reach across the front seat's threshold past
Jesus's hand—which is enveloped in God's—

to turn on the radio. God pushes his thumb
through the hole in her hand with the same
force Deniece Williams pushes out a note:

Oh, love, oh, love, stop making a fool of me,
He belts to Jesus because singing is the closest
some men come to crying. I cannot say

anything else. The night ripples through us.

A WOMAN LOVINGLY STROKES HER LOVER'S ARM IN THE BOOKSTORE BECAUSE THEY'RE IN LOVE

And I taste the blood pooling from the blister
in my mouth. And I am a jar

of names not worthy of repeating. I want
to hold you in our sickness, apply

the vapor rub to your feet. I can never write
a love poem that doesn't end

with death so here is a list of the dead: Jackie,
Franklin, Maria . . . And I remember

my grandparents were divorced decades before
I entered the world.

Please God, don't let me slip
into the persona. The heater warms us, though the past

due bill hangs on the refrigerator
like a report card, a loose tooth, an ancestor we know

has met the wrong side of a rope.
I find it ironic that my grandmother's maiden name

was Valentine. What to do with the song
in my heart that hasn't been softened

by a hand not my own? Should I accept
the hand of someone who views me as a chore?

Most days I rebuke
myself, a pile of unclean laundry unfolding

on a newly carpeted floor.

ALL THE MEN I LOVE

carry   a sweetness: reluctance,   a voice laced

with honey,   anything   society deems   ordinary   on   a woman.

My father was   a soft violence   taken   by a softer violence

the size of a golf ball.   The night remembers a blooming fist,   the way he held   the bottle

like an oyster   holds   an intruder against   its fleshiest parts. We remember the way he battered

fish   as the kitchen sweat,   which is to say   we've constructed   a better   version

of   the truth.   Last week,   in the backyard,   I listened

to the wrinkled man   interrupting   the woman   trapped in the speakerbox

as he sang   Happy Birthday   to   the woman in the yellow dress.   The seasoned

brain matter   of crawfish   plops   on the faded newspaper   in my lap   as someone

lights   the cake's candles.   The music,   which I don't remember   now, is soaked

with a story   about a girl in love   with a   false version   of the truth. We watch

the woman   surround   her cake and I'm reminded   that everyone   I love   is dying.

ALL DAY WE'VE BEEN SPEAKING IN THE DARK

for my friends, Kingston, NY, 2019

and all day the bay horses graze.
We are happy.
We snore. We stain a dish
with mixed-berry marmalade.
What if I stopped here? What if we all did?
          We are all happy and snore like overworked fathers
and damaged mothers. Everything is a thick kilt
pushed over the eyes. I might be wrong when I think
all anyone anticipates is living. But are you alright?
I crave quality fruit, ache for overbuttered popcorn, porcupines
without the stick. We are all so formal in our wantings.
We whisper-walk down wooden hallways. We grow so hard
we are dying.
          We are all happy and snore into each chamber
of ourselves. The bay horses hide our dreams in the barn.
We do not grab them from their maws. Our mothers
are damaged and our fathers brew. Inheritance, a kettle
crying *hamartia*. The water burns honeybush. Oh, God
how the spoons chatter. The way you shake in your sleep
when you think the train has hit you. The police will not
break the door. The windows are open. We'll sing arrows
into them. We are the commonwealth of hooded children
in loud raincoats stealing a porch hammock. We trouble
the Gregory Pecks down the lane and bust open the chests
of neighbors' chifforobes looking for Tom Robinson.
It is too late for us to own the mouths of our own
darkness. We can't be free, we live here.

AFTER THE 1916 FILM

The Realization of a Negro's Ambition requires melatonin & the soft dying body of a monkey face orchid.

The brilliant strangeness of watching everyone not you grow comfortable with themselves.

Trying to rehabilitate one or multiple racists.

Learning death does not fear you.

I am afraid of stars. The sky is a womb that allows for reentry.

Can you teach me how to rest? I know there are different avenues to happy but I still choose this one.

I've had panic attacks since I was five.

Everything you fear keeps you alive.

I am not safe inside the vehicle nor when I reach the tenor. Neglect, a different type of death. I mean here I am in the center of my body leaning left over exhausting myself.

I am a life skill. I am a body who loves the mercy of movement.

Tell me what to do specifically. I'd like some guidance.

I scare away all the punctuation

I am a sentence that is not allowed to end

I'M ALWAYS SO SERIOUS

and I've decided to be kind to Faith
because she has a dead mother, and I
too will lose a parent in the next month.
I find it fucked up that her mother named
her Faith, praised her God for giving her a
breathing child only to die pressed against
the armored truck, flung and flying through glass.
My father too flew through clear glass after
the chemo took his balance while the knot
on his left lung conjured the pneumonia.
Luckily, he only shattered the living
room table. Every day, I feel like God
watches me through a viewfinder whispering,
It'll be worse next time. It'll be your mother.

THE MAPLE LEAF PIANO SPEAKS TO THE BAYOU MAHARAJAH

for James Booker (1939–1983)

The stage is a red face
of wrinkles and you've returned
from Nice with no record deal.
The first time you vomited
on me I forgave you, wore it
like a brown dressing
from Commander's Palace.
The second time you spilled,
blood swarmed
the cracks of my keys,
but you continued playing
in the slush. You backwards
Moses. I know it's not the way
you wanted to mark me
but what do you have
left to give but the remains
of a sour stomach? I created you
to glorify me, to show the world
an addict in a wig could rattle
my body with *divine imagination*.
I handed you a soul that could not
be taken by anyone who fears
you. Booker, I want it back.

12-YEAR-OLD HARRY CONNICK JR. SPEAKS TO JAMES BOOKER

I thought you released spiders
on the keys to mess with me.
I'm sorry about the tape recorder.
I wanted to hold your voice
to my ear like a secret.
Is it heroin or the police
this time? Your voice floods
the living room and I pour
it on the piano like gasoline.
You play "Malagueña,"
and the dam of me breaks
like a voice. *I've played*
Chopin's Études, I've done
the whole thing, I want you
to teach me. My dad doesn't
care, come back when you're sober.
I picked up the phone when
I shouldn't have. *Harry, come*
get me. I'm getting beat up by the police.
You'd cry and I would just
lull and talk and lull. I kept toying
with the recorder
like a rosary,
like a light switch,
like any little thing
you could worry in the dark.

JAMES BOOKER SPEAKS TO RINGO STARR ABOUT HIS BODYGUARD TAKING HIS EYE

You made a stranger
perform your own
tantrum. Don't be
embarrassed. I'm
still here. Where I am from,
a man is judged if he cannot
finish what he started, so
finish me. Show me
how you fight and I'll
show you how to possess
Chopin and turn him
into something darker
than his own shadow.
Little Lazarus, why wasn't it you
who yanked the song
out of me? I blessed
the bloody knuckle
with the percussion
you could not make.
The fist that was not
yours formed into a furious
tumor, a fat flounder
forcing its living against
the brown swamp
of my face. You made sure
I was opened properly. If you
were a real man, you would've
let me feed your hunger
in an easier way, would've
let me teach you Fats Domino
with one hand
held over my gaping

left socket while the other hand
danced among the ivories.
Instructor of the obedient,
I see you. We both call
others to move for us,
both own heavy
hands that draw blood
from the objects
we wish to be.

A FUNERAL ENDING WITH BEYONCÉ

for Tracie and Aryanna

When Tracie shows us her bloated
pointer finger, there is no ponderosa near so I
knock my chest until redness comes down
the palm and God sends me every animal
to pray with. She thinks she'll die this time,
from the cat's bite. The infection is spreading
to the shoulder, though it is only the finger
that shows her sickness, fat and tan as
the belly of a roadrunner. Tracie decides Aryanna
and I should emcee her funeral: It will be in
New Mexico under the watchful eyes of ponderosa
pines who'll coat her casket with the scent
of vanilla. Frybread is to be waiting on every
chair and I imagine my mother there holding
my speech so the grease from the bread doesn't
bleed through the index cards. She'll remind me
that when her father died, everyone forgot
he was struck by lightning as a young man.
I'll forget to tell her I've been recording
our conversations so I can carry her
voice miles away from where she sleeps.
I stiffen at the thought of her death and knock
on the ponderosa, its bark redder than the amputated
finger Tracie made us promise to put in the pocket
of her dress—a lonely fire extinguisher that created
the fire. The mourners finish their bread and I jump
in the casket with her. Aryanna shakes
her head as she turns on the stereo to play
"I Was Here." Who would the living be
without the dead in the ground?

WE WEAR EACH OTHER'S NAMES

after reading If Beale Street Could Talk *and* The Odyssey

I. Fonny recast as Odysseus

> *He knows that he must do something to keep himself*
> *from drowning in this place, and every day he tries.*
> James Baldwin

I understand   the liquor in us

We are   away   seizing

each other's throats   stomaching all the bitters

and here you are   an audience   making me

                    a boy   waiting

to wife   the eye of want   again

Stop turning the pages   Don't reposition your antennas

Mold me out of the hollow that governs   my joy

            to the mouth of rest

                            The water fights me over

and over while

            Penelope bathes him in a tub of big water

            that   babbles his name

        I am every tongue

                            my son learned to use

in the lack of me

                my son   come

    seek   a ship that survives its trip home

    call   it mercy

II. Alonzo Jr. recast as Telemachus, Age 21

The baby asked,
"Is there not one righteous among them?"
James Baldwin

Is there an ethics to mythmaking?
Is there a family that imagination is not allowed to touch?
Fonny wanted to build Tish a table. To remain the center,
my father tried to run me over. A wound is a bare patch
of grass on which a baby's head falls. A plow that parts
the earth like a rat tail comb. I hold my father's absence
because it is the blade of my becoming. I twist
my wrist so every vein is upright and exposed. Do you see
me bleeding in the way only children can?
In what way would *you* like to be devastated? I already know
the color of my own tenderness. Yours is next to mine tracing
diamonds around the television. Breathing
is a tender type of breaking. A myth is just someone bathing
a boy in water not yet made from weeping.

III. Tish recast as Penelope

And now again the stormwinds have caught away
my beloved son.

Homer

I say I live in a shushing (a woman waiting while a hero is out). Can you tell me it doesn't hurt to live here? Can you return to (for) me, silence me out of witnessing my selves: unmistakably American (I stab the onions), I wash a boy's hair in a warehouse fashioned into love, sleep (I never do this). You are the toy civilian perched in the glass window, your bow an arm stuck flexing. I am the hand that paddles your parting. You are the shape *without* makes around the body.

moiety is an arrow campaigning for

                                 our

    now

          all the world

                                                    the water

and just like   the water

                              these throats

        want you dead

I say I live in a shushing

                    a hero out   while

Can you tell me it doesn't hurt to live here?

return to   for me

silence me out of witnessing my selves:

                              I stab

I never   do this

moiety an arrow campaigning for
                                   our
   now
        all the world

                                        the water

and just like   the water
                              these throats
       want you dead

MALCOLM'S SONG

Malcolm is always a hoarse singer.
        I once learned he loved Billie Holiday.

He won't dance, but he knows how
        he'll die:

My Malcolm cries out to Betty but only the wilderness
        responds. My Malcolm sings on a crowded bus,

the wind slapped from his lungs, but he still gives
        the black woman riding alone

a decent serenade. He doesn't sing from the hole
        the Nation slingshotted into his neck, he's all

diaphragm and crooner and "Stand by Me" in a brown
        trench coat, a fired member of the rat pack

that out-Sinatra'd Sinatra, too militant for gentrified
        sound. My Malcolm had to be replaced with Sammy.

If you ask him about it, he doesn't have hard feelings,
        Sometimes pain is good. It focuses you.

Let me focus on you and sing you a song. His laugh is the
        exhale of an oversized engine at a red light. The girl tells

Red to go 'head, sing his song. The words overflow from his dead
        mouth, wet with precision and immutable

praise of night: *No, I won't be afraid. I won't cry, darlin'.*
        Darling Malcolm nervously proposes to Betty Sanders

over telephone: His voice breaks. The song
        Betty knows. God knows the song

will be longer than his life. This love: a black woman
        who knows time will sorrow them.

POEM AT THE END OF THE WORLD (OR LAST WEEK'S DREAM)

We sit here eating his depression
cupcakes instead of the small
slices of tiramisu and pomegranate
he promised us
but it is okay,
our professor is dying,
as are the rest of us,
and he doesn't want us to die
hungry so the moment is still
beautiful. The end of the world
extends a broken arm
to our building, Gus gets up
and shuts the blinds. The classroom
window coats with a color we cannot
see or we pretend not to
or maybe it's just me.
I sit with my back to the window
on the 12th floor, the brackish water is rising,
and brown pelicans are choking
on the heads of bass.
Everything I love stands with death
at its heels so let me just tell you the truth:
I am bitter. I do not get to leave
at the hands of a sickness
I thought would take me first: asthma,
anxiety, OCD, an infection of the finger
that would result from my OCD because
I wash my hands so much they raw
and bleed. I did not undercook the chicken
or die from salmonella. I did not get arrested
for doing something exceptionally black
like voting for a black woman who scares

Republicans shitless so my afro has been a waste.
There has never been a gas leak in the apartment
and I restocked the toilet paper because
there is a possibility I may come back
as a ghost and my ghost-self may have
the same stomach issues as my flesh-self.
I sit with my back to the window, and I still remember
the name of my childhood best friend. I sit with my back
to the window and our professor asks if he did
a good job making dessert, his eyes red from exhaustion
or fear or guilt—most definitely fear.
You should make this again. I sit with my back
to the window and watch Gus's little girl
(no one else has brought family)
laughing, a pimple of brown frosting
on the tip of her nose. Gus, who married
a woman with hair as thick as his own,
parts her hair for the last time. We pray
the comb won't break.

OH, HOW THE GHOST OF YOU CLINGS

never

free

bound

around us

I can see

little

A cigarette   s

hea t has

foolish

tinkling

w   o   nt

A   ground

remind   you

conquer

rings   a

host

long excited

fo   r

evening

foolish

       sweet

things

          m   a

k   e

   ghost   s

Wild

        wing

      e   d

           roses

  whistling

   dear

bring   me

     the wail of

        dreamers

O , o   o o o

       you

MY PHONE AUTOCORRECTS "NIGGA" TO "NIGHT"

My nights

play cousin to

their mother's favorite

kettles. My nights won't consume

their reflections so they pour milk

in their coffee. My nights never rest

so they sing their shadows to sleep. Sometimes

they don't remember any words. My nights have frogs

stuck in their throats, no light soul, every bit of pain, my nights

all Louis Armstrong minus a trumpet and my nights play chicken

with the train. My nights both shoe and polish. Both Sambo and Bruce

Leroy. We all little pretty medallions on our grandmothers' nightstands. My nights

are mistaken for other nights that bear no resemblance. I saw the sinew of the oldest night

in the neighborhood on the floor, his saint pendant missing. All the small, down-feathered nights

scatter from the groan of pig sirens. My nights don't know their history. My nights are pecans without

the trees that grow them. My nights instruct all the people in their head to weep. My nights hate the firefly

cutting their darkness. My night, did you see them? They just walked right passed us and didn't even speak. My nights are ordinary,

wear ruffled socks, have the best belts. My nights don't always go to church, but my nights are lambs worthy

of the morning. My nights are revised constitutions, crypt keepers, my nights are a congregation

of alligators on a rumpus bayou. My nights hiss into themselves. No one hears. Their blood

rolls its eyes. My nights chew gum and sunflower seeds. My nights eat pork. My nights

get the itis and slur their speech. My nights protest protests. The government

watches. My nights live in Brazil Botswana the Congo Cuba the DR France

Grenada Greece Honduras Ireland Liberia Lithuania Nigeria Venezuela Zimbabwe. My nights live in America to remind you of me. Some people think my nights are better with their eyes closed but my nights have beautiful corneas. My nights wash clothes that don't belong to them and won't look their bosses in the eye. My nights know necessity. My nights oblige. When my nights die, I wash them on my kitchen table. After my nights are washed, I throw away the table. My nights have names. My nights smell of sage. My nights smell of the muddy rivers they will never swim in again.

AMERICA ASKS, "WHAT'S WRONG WITH YOU?"

Tell me it doesn't hurt to live in you?

BUCKJUMP

after Douglas Kearney,
for the souls of the enslaved buried near the sugar cane fields in West Baton
Rouge Parish

Everything left of the slaves is near the sugar.
We slurp the syrup after the cane.
Near the sugar, everything left of the slaves.
Come, cut the cane into caricatures.
Calculate the culture in our lips.
Calculate their capacity.

Insidious my siblings
aren't we
inaccurate in
our suffering?

We suffer more.

We buckjump

and whoop

and whoop.

We season, turn steel.

Outside, obvious: arbor, ambivalence, abhorrent poplar.

In
the poplar
the   true
sparrow
pipes
Near   the
sugar,

everything left
of the slaves.

Pint-sized precaution. Everything inside a stocking hangs
near the sugar, tell me: what is left of the slaves?

Do not slurp the syrup.
Instead, buckjump here,

in this heat.

Invest in the fade.
    Farther ahead, the long-
                haired men   then nuke it.
                      with feathers   nostalgia into a braid,
                            circumnavigate

Buckjump. Whoop. Whoop. Stomp your feet until the bouillon turns bullion.

                                    Long-haired &
                                    loyal, we saliva-
                                    soaked spirituals &
                                    Mississippi water.
                                    chant chant. We big
                                    black radios, tall
                                    tongues.

                                    jump
                                buck-
                            jump
                        buck-
                    jump
                buck-
we big black   jump   radios, tall tongues
saliva   buck-   saliva
soaked   soaked
tongues   jump   tongues

TONGUE WE BIG BLACK RADIOS, TALL TONGUES
TALL   buck jump and whoop and whoopwhoopwhoop WE BIG
          buck jump and whoop and whoopwhoopwhoop
WE BIG   buck   d whoop and whoopwhoopwhoop BLACK
BLACK   bu   whoop and whoopwhoopwhoop   RADIOS
          bu   hoop and whoopwhoopwhoop
RADIOS   bu   whoop and whoopwhoopwhoop   WE BIG
WE BIG   buck   j whoop and whoopwhoopwhoop BLACK
          buck jump and whoop and whoopwhoopwhoop
BLACK   buck jump and whoop and whoopwhoopwhoop RADIOS
RADIOS WE BIG BLACK RADIOS, TALL TONGUES

and whoop and whoop
and whoop and whoop
and whoop and whoop

I want to do right by us. I'll say it plain:
Everything left of the slaves: sugar.
Near the sugar, everything left.

The slaves' slugs move fast on a face furious
with fear. Woozy & world-worn I keep

a grill in my wallet, give myself
freedom like a white forefather.
Come, look at me whoop & jump,
my smile a beam, a pinto's buck.
To all you gladiators, I'm weary & bitter.
Worry me in my black city, come fire,
I watch you & you wither.

Everything left of me is sugar. Alabaster.
Angola. Melancholy marginalia. Momma.
Daddy. Nigga in the alley. Punctuated

southpaw. Pathological pusher man,
come calculate all that's left of me,
no sugar left in the tank. If a tall man in
blue is ready to do what he does, what
does that make me but a slave?

WHAT DO YOU HAVE LEFT TO SAY?

for Renisha McBride (1994–2013), Miriam Carey (1979–2013),
Shantel Davis (1989–2012), and Aiyana Mo'Nay Stanley-Jones (2002–2010)

What do you have left to say,

that you've grieved

     all the black men you can no longer

touch? How one-dimensional you are that you will

     water the magnolias that rupture

your father's eyes while   your mother still lives

above ground,   that you've tried to find the female

in every   man around you

and have failed.

That's fucked up, right?   That you know

     no one was there for Renisha, or Miriam, that

you've seen Shantel's face   on a shirt,

and Aiyana has been turned   into fiction.

Every now and again you look   at your mother

and ask, did you ever have   a dream?

She did.

Now that she has split herself open onto you,

     an aloe plant brandishing

cumbersome gel,   do you understand

your mistake?   You don't?

Remember the woman as black

      as God pulling

your hand away from the hot stove and you

not saying thank you? No?

Now, whose fault is that?

PERIPETEIA

I.

It has been established   from the pulled muscle,
                    the perforated ulcer,
          the perpetual lack
of persimmons   on the mantel—
          because I'd spurn
                    any other sweetness taking the rightful place
                              of mangos—that I don't take
                              kindly to change.
                    So when I did not wake
          to the fog usually surrounding me
I did not know
what to do with myself.

Clearly, I was not prepared for what normalness I prayed for.

I had no summer dresses,
no pullover sweaters,
          no parkas or pineapple-
          colored ponchos with hoods
to protect me from pouring rain.
Every purse has been slashed
by the pocketknife I own
          to cut Peruvian peppers and roughly
                                        ripe pumpkins. The pajamas,
                              ripped-up pantyhose, empty
                    porcelain perfume bottles,
          and parachute pants from last Halloween
have long been plucked
from the dresser drawers
          and replaced by gold

pinky rings, paper copies
of past-due medical bills, and
one-
piece swimsuits. Regardless, I knew
I could surely cop a cardigan,
could go out in black
wedge heels and be
pretty but I don't know how
to hold my face. This morning,
I unearthed
a violence—age 22 years and 358 days old.
My body knew before
I could stop it.

II. Today I Killed My Anxiety

I murdered // my unwanted // sister // my worst sung // spiritual // more ubiquitous // than the maker // who made me // then // summoned // my borderless dark

thirstful canary

I'm not // sorry I went // through with it // this time // you broke // all my younger // years into // serpentine slumber // I crafted // your undoing // with the butcher's blade // sweaty and crepe like a birthing pig // where can you love // now that I'm healthy // enough for slaughter

I know myself

there's no blood // in the apartment // the carpet is clean // my neighbors are not // snitches // they backed me // from their fire // escapes // drunk // with wild // ad-libs // called her a useless hoe // an extra set // of teeth // they saw me // gut the girl

I

rented // this place of prescribed // happiness // until I could move // into a villa // with my name // on the deed //

I

now own seven sets // of silvery wind chimes // two Pomeranians // I drape velvet // across the balcony // and yell // to the fullness // *Look at how soft // I have made // myself* // praise // her hard absence

I am now a good opening // I'm not trying to gloat // but as an American // I know you must // kill a thing to be // called // a hero // and I'm tired // of feeling so neo- // natal // so yes // I killed her // bump that // I blessed her // yes // like any man // who puts his hands // on a woman and calls it // love //

God was not home that night so it wasn't forbidden

THIS IS A SONG FOR THE GOOD GIRL (OR THE LONELY)

I draw a black band on my arm with Sharpie

Mourn for America they say

Say! Say Mami with the braids. I like 'em short!

My mom is the only number in my Recents call log

I now understand why Saturn devoured his son

I sleep with the TV on to combat loneliness

Today my cousin turns seven in a twice-drowned city

Every year I tell him he's a grown man

Lying runs in my family

My sister steals a graham cracker

Animal control comes to put her down

We found a gun in my dead aunt's bedroom

The silence hangs over us

like a guillotine's blade

I dream of fish and close my legs

I stopped playing the alto saxophone

The president threatens to drop a bomb

It felt too close to giving birth

The earth holds me like a dead snake in the grass

Each of my days is a failed manifesto

I clench my jaw as to hold myself

Who will Jodeci cry for me as I undo my twist out

What is a man but a pocket

full of rose thorns

They are always so afraid to bleed

I do it without being asked

III.

I'M ALWAYS SO SERIOUS

I was spoiled by lavish thoughts,
I admit it. History almost unchained itself

from my weaker clavicle.
Everyone looked

so excited on the anniversary of assassination.
I wrote this because I want to live

in the house I cannot own because
I am not white. Forgive me. I've said this

before but I was in a different state,
a softer mania, and this time, a wife lunged

towards the mouths of overwatered
magnolias. They were already dead.

At my home, two chickens peck
the yard and refuse to leave us eggs.

I refuse to rest out of unmet want.
I mean, I harass the gnats in the bathroom.

I fix the Sprite, wash your back,
watch the night, eat all the dead crab.

You watch me accumulate in particulars.
I stretch the curtains. This is daylight: the swelling

of a lizard's red throat.
Inside the home I want for the wrong reason,

there is a lamp that won't work. I know because
the owners keep their blinds open.

The husband joins his wife near the olive
shaded lamp and quails

as his raving lover seizes the neck of
the fixture. I shudder in the passenger seat of

this city, far enough to not be heard but a light shines
bright and I am seen, sleuthing and serious. I know

close violences still form in the absence of want.
I keep walking as the husband shuts the blinds.

AN ELEGY BEGINNING AND ENDING WITH A MOUSE

I let the baby mouse
live because I cannot kill
what has ears. Besides,
mice run from the rain,
burrow into warm
homes when the snow
dollops over their small
bodies. I was nine when it first
snowed in New Orleans.
My fists were and still are
small and I chose to throw them
against my cousin's mouth
when she laughed at my
unknowing of death.
We cannot start over
or take on a new body as
brilliant or as pitiful as the last
we inhabited. How I won't
remember that moment,
the way my cousin's blood
clotted the snow as it spilled
from her body. How I won't
remember my mother
is my mother after I am
lowered into the opened
earth and have failed to
one-up Lazarus. I won't
remember that little mouse,
that furry fist of ears
and eyes blacker
than omission.
How I could not kill it.

How I know if it had
a human mother,
it would already be
named. It already
looks like all of us
in its woundedness:
gray and sleeping.

AND

And the birds waiting to shit on people's heads at Broadway Junction. And the army recruiters behind the table telling black teens they can be on the other side of the gun. And the only time the airport staff is friendly is when I wear my Ivy League sweatshirt. Me being the token and liking it. And the strange man at the bus stop who wouldn't let me leave until I gave him a hug. And my white neighbors who laugh like they don't fear death. And the third time I've checked the stovetops but still can't sleep. And the heavy-handed beauticians braiding my hair. And every person who's ever asked if my hair is real. Every moment I can't cornrow. And every rat that makes its way into my apartment. And the gentrifiers. And every white congressman that represents a predominately black district. And 9th Ward second lines with nothing but white transplants in it. And the roach I found in the banana bag. And the roommate who has sex too loud and too often in our apartment. And I can never travel without a stomachache. I think I'll never have a home to come back to. And the people who wear glasses for the aesthetic. And the dreams grandmothers have that make you afraid to leave the house. And the corner of the counter my hip hits. And the ducking I do when I don't know if I've heard fireworks or gunshots. And everyone who doesn't consider Pluto a planet. Every sickness that made us lose a parent that year.

AMERICA ASKS, "WHAT'S WRONG WITH YOU?"

Everything, but that is my business.

AMPLE

EXT. THE BLACK BOOK/BOOK OF BLACKNESS — MIDDAY

There is ample.
Ample is here.
        A girl making lemon cake.
She made a lemon cake. There is ample.
Ample cake.
        Shoulders up
        and down.

Cicely Tyson holds the tongue of Paul Robeson reciting his role, but better.

        A "blues"?

        A yesno?

Girl

My book is   Book   a weapon
no matter   how I hold it.
I show the   darkness:

                            Book

       book

   book

Why the ▮ always?

Girl

I write to ███████.
I keep a promise to ████████.

The Darkness

You write to ██?

INT. THE CHURCH OF BLACK BOOKS/BOOKS OF BLACKNESS — KITCHEN

There is ample.
Ample is here.
              A girl stirring cake batter.

She's preparing a lemon cake.
Ample thickness. Thickness is ample.

INT. THE CHURCH OF BLACK BOOKS/BOOKS OF BLACKNESS — PULPIT

              Ample praise.

       S   I   N   G   into the ample.

Cicely Tyson holds the tongue of Paul Robeson.

(
W
o
m
e
n

This is ample:

a ring around the eye

a ligament

d
r
e
s
s
e
d

i
n

t
h
e
i
r

S
u
n
d
a
y

B
e
s
t

f
a
i
n
t

at the pinkness of it.)

A church hat flies. Next, a hornet's nest.

> I write to the Guinness World Records.

> I rewrite The Green Book.

EXT. AMPLE CITY — EVENING

Everything, a RING around the eye.

Everything, a LIGAMENT.

The ample city applauds a poet's return. They participate in holy action.

> Liquor is ample. Cue the spirit of Dionysus.

BEGIN MONTAGE:

> —Tractors pulling a wheeled float.

> —Dark children dressed like poets. In watching: little sugars shining.

> —Looters lose themselves in arrest.

> —Catahoula hounds stir.

Everything, a RING around the eye.

Everything, a LIGAMENT.

EXT. IPPI WATER — NIGHT

The children plunging. There is ample.

Ample cake (Cake. Cake ample with lemon). Bitter orchard. Barricade the caravan. Catahoula hounds coping. Carnivores at Carnival. Cleaver. Coronation. Cicely Tyson cradling the breath of Cicely Tyson. Dionysus dining on a plastic grape. Damnation. Disqualification. Disenfranchisement is a white invention. Educated, Enunciate. Everything. EKG machine. Empty earache. Famous falsetto. Frottoir. FUBAR. Fasciitis. Field mice in the fight.

Can you honor you? me?

you > me

Praise the ample:

Ample Ample Alice Coltrane, $\dfrac{me}{you}$ harp in hand, drinks the Tabasco.

Cicely Tyson holds herself. A LEMON CAKE Alice holds the knife.
sits in between the
two.

They give an education.

                                                  They make a seat.

They count their money.

Girl

There aren't any people watching my back
is tender.

Ample exits.

EXIT. THE. MISS. RIVER — NIGHT

There is ample. American Ampleness drowned the dark children

quivering in the pull string river

spine in hand.

River speaks: *Don't let me push you*. Says,

COME EXPERIENCE AMPLE!

COME ANXIOUS IN THE AMPLE!

AGGRESSIVE you, Ample is ours

INT. GIRL

Just arrived

Don't let Cicely Tyson leave.

Let me teach us how to breathe

: *in*   **; incorrectly**

: There is ample, etc. :   ; The children have drowned ;

: There is ample :   ; We don't sleep
enough ;

                 I should make lemon cake

: I made lemon cake :

: There is ample :

: Ample cake :

                                  ; shoulders up and down ;

                No more cake

                                  ; Ample exits ;

                The phone rings

: The phone is a slingshot :

: The phone is answered :

: Listening is ample :

                Hello, Ample?

: Ample's aunt asks for Ample :

                The car, nothing but a radio.

                                  ; Maxwell stops pleading
                                  through the speakers with the
                                  voice of a good son ;

                                  ; I speak ;

                I'm sorry, Logic
                Ample is over

: There is ample, rummaging
the fridge for freezer-burned
butter :

nonhuman thing weeping
at the skylight.

The sky
Eagles reimagined

: I speak: *Ample,*
apologize to Logic :

The night is not over

12:47

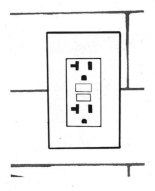

: My body a bookmark
suspended on its side :

Ample Angry

Ample,

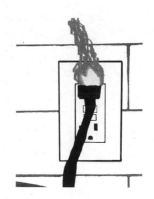

I knew it
I get up
I check

: There is ample :
Crying on all the freezer-burned
butter :

; Ample
Taps
And taps
And taps
The wall tile ;

forgot the special ingredient
to his lemon cake recipe

nonhuman thing weeping

the eggs open on the counter

: I twist off his tongue
Give him my best
And tell him to
Pull down his life :

DEMETER, REIMAGINED AS A BLACK WOMAN, SPEAKS TO PERSEPHONE

Please do not come back to me
suspended in the sky's quiet

diorama, or in umber pieces
that require me to hold the seeds

of you in my fingers
like an examiner holds

a tooth to an X-ray. Baby, I have broken
the trees for you. I will curse every

person that yells, "A man was lynched
yesterday," but refuses to acknowledge

his wife. Did they ever cut her down or
does she still swing above us like a broken

promise? What of the mothers afraid of being
mothers of daughters and fear the feathered

kiss of suffering? I asked God
for mercy. There was no answer.

I've decided you don't have to answer
me either. Because I love you, surrender

to the only darkness heavier than sleep.
Do not come back from it.

I'M ALWAYS SO SERIOUS

Old enough to know I cannot continue living
in metaphor, I tell you I want to exist
without interference. I exist with white
and static stars bursting in the center of my vision.
It is after the concussion. I fear I may go blind.
We sit unfastened on the long back of the bridge
eating the curled bodies of fried squid in the train
car, sharing the fork. Beyond the laminated glass,
the air is the overwhelming color of doves. You've
canceled your date with the bank teller to chaperone
me to a room the color of absence where a flashlight
beams into my already expanded pupils.
You say, *It's fine*, you and your boy wouldn't work out.
He refused to say bless you when I sneezed. I ask you how
you're going to celebrate Black History Month now
and you say by staying alive. You say you have
a German shepherd whose nails need trimming,
a humidifier that needs distilled water, and you need
a manicure that you'll get tomorrow because
it is already 7:30 and the snow is unrelenting.
In the winters when I am the only one
in New York besides the family I've handpicked,
my mother checks weather patterns. Even after
protest, she mails me jam, thermals, and every
packaged and precooked thing that survives
each postal worker it is passed to. I tell her to
save her money. As always, she refuses.

There should be a safe word for this kind
of kindness. Friend, look, across from us:
there is a couple whose hair is a coiled collection
of clouds covering their peripherals. They hover
over the beaded head of their child in what I can't
distinguish is a whisper or kiss—doesn't matter
because when you roll your eyes in their direction,
they have stopped their surrender. Friend, don't let me
interrupt your living. Let me
tell you this while the metal carries us:
I care that you are cared for. You've watched
the cuff squeeze my arm. It is Valentine's
Day. We know that mostly everything around us
is measured in blood. I am holding your hand
after the concussion to steady myself and the
constellations that make themselves known.
The subway whooshes us over the buildings dressed
in white coats. We sit in the *clack clack* of movement.

GHOSTS

On the J train, the boy who just learned to feed
himself yells *look mommy, I'm dead* and no one
hears but me. No one else watches his jaw widen

to give his brother room to shoot more ghost
bullets in his mouth. The soggy pieces of bread
still rest like cotton crusted against his gums.

Just this morning I watched my ghost
father through the coffee shop window.
He pushed his newly ghosted brother

in a stolen wheelchair from the clinic
across the street. My uncle, who misses
himself, traded in his flesh foot for hospital

purchased nothingness: the off-brown plastic
connected to the hole in his knee. Both wore
a suit of spoons. I waved and both chimeras

ran from the security team spilling from the mouth
of emergency room doors. My father smiled, flung
them both into traffic. Their spoons shimmered like

flames swallowing an unattended child's hand,
our reflections spiraling into the cars—ourselves
crushed against our metal selves.

We are at dinner when the two-year-old
my cousin has given birth to says,
I'll call the police on you if you don't

get my fries. And he says it as a joke, but
I know death is an infection that will loosen
him from the gum of the Earth.

I'm certainly scared the responder will listen,
lapping up the sweetness of his baby voice
filling the phone like molasses through a town.

WHEN COMPARING YOUR HANDS TO YOUR FATHER'S

consider how one set has harmed your mother
and the other vows to never touch a man
that's not half dead on the living room floor.
If heaven exists, which set is cruel enough to be God?

The other has vowed to never touch a broken man
who hums louder than a shaking heater at night.
Which God is cruel enough to let heaven exist
beyond the border of an uncharted silence?

He is a shaking heater humming loud tonight
going through your mother's black leather
purse. The quarters sing in his hands slashing silence.
His hands push the change to his chest patriotically.

Your mother is black and goes through
the living room threshold: your father half dead on the floor,
the EMT's hands pushing the defibrillator against his chest.
Consider how much your mother wants to harm them all.

A WOMAN YELLS, "MAXINE!" 14 TIMES OUTSIDE MY BROOKLYN WINDOW

Please Lord, let it be
a dog dead in the street
and not a woman black
as me. Today was a good
day. I drowned my hash browns
in a plate of ketchup and David Ruffin
sang about the bees' envy. I rode
the subway without complaining
today and there was no delay
after crossing the Brooklyn Bridge.
The only crimes I witnessed
were the solid-built man refusing
to rise and let the old woman sit
on the hard plastic of subway seat,
and the white woman who was bold
enough to leave her apartment
with "dreadlocks" tangling out her scalp.
Today, I almost forgot
that I was far away from my mother
and her growing hands that would grease
the driest parts of my scalp without being
asked to. Today, I almost forgot
that anyone who doesn't share my face
would care if I went missing. Maxine
should be the name of a Jack Russell
or a retriever that has escaped
its leash and run into the street
for some type of wet freedom
nothing else but the rain offers.
I know nothing of pet ownership
but I know what it is like to fear
the night and every lost thing
that can get precious in it.

I'M ALWAYS SO SERIOUS

The Golden Shovel

All the continents now pulled apart by Earth's knowledge of us, we
are a silent choir of buzzing in different hemispheres. A knife cuts at our combs and the both of us reel
back into our honeys. I know we both cool
and warm the floors of oceans with our light. We,
the carriers of our lungs, could have moved to any country you wanted, left
the land of greedy mouths and childish things to tour every blade of wheat and build a school
for our troubles where we teach them to sleep. We,
the unalarmed and unconcerned for anyone who isn't us, show the children how to breathe in the hours of lurking,
break open the eggs of robins and prepare breakfast late.
Here, give me the gun, and I'll blade open the head of a coconut so we
have the meat of something worth striking,
never having to explain to your parents and set the story straight.
Who are you to step into grief and not apologize? Twe-
nty-three and human. Listen to us: me, tough, and you, good, sing
with all our teeth and then softly, like the spot on an infant's head or anything else sin
can create. Of course, of course. We-
ariness is a wire and reason. Of course we'll all disturb the earth at the end of our thin
lives when called, and begin
our stay in the ground. We-
eping, the cicadas buckle their ribs into a tremendous jazz
and give me another reason to hate June.
But there is now winter on the leaves and we
are aware that the arrival of everything unsteadies
you. Your body not yet heavy with dew. The air not yet birthing the inevitable monsoon.

CAN'T AFFORD SADNESS IN A TIME LIKE THIS

Because no one is down sick or dead
tired, the black patron saint of sadness

tells me I'm not allowed to weep.
So here I am, all manners and no accent,

sitting here in the land of field peas and saltwater
fish, not weeping, but watching

my cousin in Act I of motherhood
as she pulls the pink taffy from her fingers

and stuffs it in her twins' mouths. They stretch
their necks like stunted giraffes. We can't afford

sadness on this wide street of abandoned
school buses where we both stole

our first sip of Crown, where a neighbor boy crashed
my cousin's dirt bike into the tree and she cursed him

out like a drunk uncle
until her mother dragged her

into the house. We can't afford it
as we sit in the foliage of willows. We must

enjoy a gentle sweat. The leaves
are so green and cover us both

like Baptist hands, no one hears us
sing of our no-show siblings with a Motown

grief. No one can look at us and know
we are as lonely as every room

without a piano. We know too
much and not enough about

our faces and who gave them to us.
My father now lives

in the letters on my cousin's calf
and I visit him when I can.

Her father joined him this year,
and I have not offered my skin

as a canvas for a needle's pinch. I know
they both went into a light, my father breathing,

until not. Her father breathing then thrashing
into it like their pet pit hit

by the mail truck. Her puppies left
to house in their peeling garage.

I've been running from what needs me.
I refuse to make either of us cry in this poem so

I'll just tell you that the willow weeps.

POEM NOTES

The epigraph "Da Souf got sum to say" comes from the speech André 3000 made at the 1995 Source Awards after Outkast won Best New Rap Group. There are many ways this quote has been written. After reading the August 6, 2018, Uproxx article, "'Da Souf Got Sum To Say': On The Willful Mistranslation Of André 3000's Famous Line" by Alex Ashford, I have decided to use the spelling that Ashford uses so as not to erase the natural dialect of my fellow southerner André 3000 (https://uproxx.com/music/andre-3000-mistranslation-da-souf-got-some-to-say/).

"Self-Portrait" is after the poem "Self-Portrait With & Without" by Chen Chen.

"Things That Fold" is after the poem "Things That Break" by Jamaal May.

The C. J. Peete Public Housing Development was the official name of the Magnolia Housing Projects located in the uptown area of New Orleans, Louisiana, where my family is from. The Magnolia was demolished three years post-Katrina in 2008, and the area is now home to the Harmony Oaks Apartments. The poem is dedicated to Ms. Cheryldale V. Washington, a close family friend who I consider an aunt, and one of the people I interviewed when I planned on making a short documentary about family and friends who lived in the Magnolia pre-Katrina. This documentary was never finished, but the italicized words in this poem are her words and come from my interview with her.

"Jesus is so quiet" contains lyrics from the song "Silly" by Deniece Williams.

"After the 1916 Film" was written after reading the plot summary of the 1916 short film *The Realization of a Negro's Ambition* in the book *The 50 Most Influential Black Films: A Celebration of African-American Talent, Determination, and Creativity* by S. Torriano Berry and Venise T. Berry (Citadel Press, 2001). *The Realization of a Negro's Ambition*, directed by Harry A. Gant, was a silent film (its footage is now lost) whose main character's ambitions were realized after saving a white woman.

"The Maple Leaf Piano Speaks to the Bayou Maharajah," "12-Year-Old Harry Connick Jr. Speaks to James Booker," and "James Booker Speaks to Ringo Starr about His Bodyguard Taking His Eye" are in memory of the genius New Orleans musician James Booker (1939–1983). James Booker was one of the, if not the, best piano players to ever come from New Orleans. While he was a musical genius, society's homophobia and racism, and his personal struggles with mental illness and drug addiction, were major factors in his untimely death. This is the start to what I hope to be many more poems about his life. Most of my research and knowledge of James Booker's life comes from watching the 2013 documentary *Bayou Maharajah: The Tragic Genius of James Booker*, directed by Lily Keber.

"The Maple Leaf Piano Speaks to the Bayou Maharajah" has a line that paraphrases Isaiah 43:7. Divine imagination is in italics in the poem because I have taken it from a quote from Booker in the documentary: "Music is actually a divine product. So, whatever song I sing—I don't care what the message is—it's a product of my imagination, and my imagination is the result of divine imagination."

"12-Year-Old Harry Connick Jr. Speaks to James Booker" contains both altered and direct quotes from Connick from the Keber documentary. Connick Sr. was the District Attorney of Orleans Parish (1973–2003), and Booker became a close family friend to the Connicks. Allegedly, he tutored Connick Jr. at the piano in exchange for a revoked prison sentence.

James Booker wore a black eye patch with a star covering his missing left eye. He told many "stories" on how his eye was lost, one of them being that it was lost after a fight with Ringo Starr's bodyguard.

Lazarus was a nickname given to Ringo Starr due to his chronic illnesses as a child.

"A Funeral Ending with Beyoncé" references the song "I Was Here" by Beyoncé.

The epigraphs in "We Wear Each Other's Names" are from James Baldwin's *If Beale Street Could Talk* and Homer's *The Odyssey*. When reading both books, I saw a connection between Odysseus and Fonny: both men are separated from their families due to circumstances out of their control—Odysseus being lost at sea and away from

Penelope and his son Telemachus, and Fonny (Alonzo Sr.) being falsely accused of a crime due to his race and away from his fiancée Tish while she is pregnant with their son Alonzo Jr. I blend both books together and have recast *The Odyssey* with the black characters from *If Beale Street Could Talk*.

"Malcolm's Song" contains lyrics from the song "Stand by Me" by Ben E. King.

"Oh, How the Ghost of You Clings" is an erasure of the song "These Foolish Things" by Ella Fitzgerald.

"My Phone Autocorrects 'Nigga' to 'Night'" contains an altered version of the line "They were living in America to remind you of me" from the poem "Default Mode" by John Ashbery.

Buckjumping is the name of a dance performed at New Orleans second line parades. These second lines are held for jazz funerals, weddings, and any other moments worthy of celebration. The dance can be steeped in both joy and heartbreak. The poem "Buckjump" was inspired after reading the February 5th, 2017, online article on *The Advocate* website entitled "Researcher maps hidden graveyards of slaves who once tilled Louisiana sugar cane fields" by Terry L. Jones (https://www.theadvocate. com/baton_rouge/news/communities/westside/article_7f0fd2e8-e966-11e6-91bd-7b5708a1dc45.html). Genealogist Debbie Martin devotes her time to finding the identities of the black people (many of whom were enslaved) buried in forgotten and hidden cemeteries in West Baton Rouge Parish. According to the article, in addition to restoring these graves, "her mission is expanding into forming a nonprofit association she intends to use to bring respect to these burial sites and to provide younger generations with knowledge of the past." I dedicate this poem to the souls of the black people buried without the proper respect they deserved. I intend for this poem to be a written form of "buckjumping" to honor the dead and use the poem's sonic play to mimic the lively feeling of being at a New Orleans second line. In addition to the poem's sonic play, the radio-shaped typography was inspired after reading *The Black Automaton* by Douglas Kearney, and this poem also references lyrics from the song "Pusherman" by Curtis Mayfield.

"What Do You Have Left to Say?" is dedicated to Renisha McBride, murdered November 2, 2013; Miriam Carey, murdered October 3, 2013; Shantel Davis, murdered June 14, 2012; and Aiyana Mo'Nay Stanley-Jones, murdered May 16, 2010.

"This is a Song for the Good Girl (or the Lonely)" takes its title from lyrics in the song "Mine" by Beyoncé, featuring Drake, and the song "(This is) A Song for the Lonely" by Cher.

The opening line of "I'm Always so Serious [*I was spoiled by lavish thoughts*]" are lyrics from the song "Higgs" by Frank Ocean.

"Demeter, Reimagined as a Black Woman, Speaks to Persephone" references the flag that read "A Man Was Lynched Yesterday" that hung from the NAACP headquarters from 1920 until 1938 any time a lynching would occur. The item titled "The NAACP Flag" in the *NAACP: A Century in the Fight for Freedom* exhibition on the Library of Congress's website explains that "the threat of losing its lease forced the NAACP to discontinue the practice in 1938" (http://www.loc.gov/exhibits/naacp/the-new-negro-movement.html#obj8).

"I'm Always so Serious: The Golden Shovel" uses the Golden Shovel form developed by Terrance Hayes. Each line's last word spells out the poem "We Real Cool" by Gwendolyn Brooks.

This book took around six years (honestly, my whole life so far) to write. I have read many poems, pieces of fiction, nonfiction, articles, texts, listened to music, watched films, and been in community with so many others while writing this collection. I cannot remember every piece of art or person that may have informed it. To those that were in my subconscious and unrecognized here in the notes, I apologize and thank you for your existence.

ACKNOWLEDGMENTS

I express extreme gratitude to the editors of the following journals, where these poems first appeared, sometimes in different forms:

4x4 Magazine: "Prelude to Separation"

The Adroit Journal: "Can't Afford Sadness in a Time like This"

American Chordata: "Peripeteia"

Cotton Xenomorph: "A Woman Yells, 'Maxine!' 14 Times Outside My Brooklyn Window"

Four Way Review: "Things That Fold"

Glass: A Journal of Poetry: "What Do You Have Left to Say?" (published as "The Poet's Conscience Speaks")

LEVELER: "This is a Song for the Good Girl (or the Lonely)"

Luna Luna Magazine: "Demeter, Reimagined as a Black Woman, Speaks to Persephone"

Narrative: "The Month before Your Father Goes to Prison" (published as "July, 2008") and "An Elegy Beginning and Ending with a Mouse"

Pigeon Pages: "A Woman Lovingly Strokes Her Lover's Arm in the Bookstore Because They're in Love" and "A Funeral Ending with Beyoncé"

Poetry: "My Phone Autocorrects 'Nigga' to 'Night'"

The Southampton Review: "We Wear Each Other's Names"

Southeast Review: "And" and "I'm Always so Serious [*I was spoiled by lavish thoughts*]"

Southern Indiana Review: "Poem at the Ed of the World (Or Last Week's Dream)" and "All Day We've Been Speaking in the Dark"

Tilted House Review: "I'm Always so Serious: The Golden Shovel"

Tinderbox Poetry Journal: "I'm Always so Serious [which is to say in the winters I dream]" and "Jesus is so quiet"

Vinyl Poetry and Prose: "C. J. Peete, Magnolia 2004"

wildness: "All the Men I Love" (published as "Reflections After Attending a Birthday Party")

Zócalo Public Square: "What's It Like Escaping Something Trying to Kill You?"

I'd like to acknowledge that the following poems: "Self-Portrait," "All Day We've Been Speaking in the Dark," "I'm Always so Serious [and I've decided to be kind to Faith]," and "We Wear Each Other's Names" were all finalists for the 2019 Manchester Poetry Prize.

A broadside of my poem "Things That Fold" (originally published in *Four Way Review*) was reprinted and published as one of five poetry broadsides created by Antenna (Press Street) in New Orleans for their forthcoming *Reflections on Water* portfolio.

"My Phone Autocorrects 'Nigga' to 'Night'" was anthologized in *Best New Poets 2021* and was awarded the J. Howard and Barbara M. J. Wood Prize by the Poetry Foundation in 2020.

My poem "A Woman Yells, 'Maxine!' 14 Times Outside My Brooklyn Window" was a *Best of the Net Anthology* 2019 Poetry Winner (originally published in *Cotton Xenomorph*).

My poems "This is a Song for the Good Girl (or the Lonely)" and "A Woman Yells, 'Maxine!' 14 Times Outside My Brooklyn Window" were included in the exhibition *The Emotional Brain: An Exhibition Exploring Mental Health* at the Carroll Gallery in the Newcomb Art Department at Tulane University (August 23–October 22, 2021).

There are so many people I need to thank for this book coming to fruition. First and foremost, I'd like to thank my family. My parents, for meeting as children, and being the best tellers of stories. You are the first poets. To my aunts, uncles, sibling, play siblings, cousins, play cousins, everyone in the family who doesn't quite know what I do but are proud of me for writing, I thank you. To Tahj, the smallest of us who is learning how to read and is already better than us at everything: I'm sorry I couldn't play with you every time you came over. I was working on this! I hope it impresses you one day.

My homie, my ride or die, my partner in crime, Kwame Opoku-Duku III, thank you for being one of my biggest supporters and the best hype man of all time. The best thing Columbia ever did was put us in a creative writing class together. Love you, my friend.

To my writing teachers at Columbia: Emily Fragos, Marni Ludwig, Rickey Laurentiis, Timothy Donnelly, Dorothea Lasky, and Deborah Paredez (whose class I took five times and would continue to take if I still could). Morgan Parker, thank you for telling me I didn't have to write so formally and that everything didn't have to be in a complete sentence. I get it now.

To Dorla McIntosh, the HBIC, the ruler of everything. The creative writing department would be nothing without you. Thank you for your constant support and love through these years.

To my teachers at NYU: Deborah Landau, Catherine Barnett, Sharon Olds, Kimiko Hahn, Eileen Myles. My thesis advisor Terrance Hayes, my favorite two-watch wearer and poetry kin who saw this book when it was only a thesis, thank you for constantly encouraging me to tap into my inner strangeness and not hesitate. Love and light to you always.

To Malcolm Tariq, Menna Elsayed, Sasha Debevec-McKenney, and Erika Meitner, who were also some of the first readers of this book.

To my classmates and other wonderful writers I was in community with while writing the book: Bernard Ferguson, Kyle Carrero Lopez, Omotara James, Maggie Dapogny,

Crystal Valentine, Wo Chan, India Lena González, Gbenga Adesina, Sarina Romero, Nancy Huang, Melissa Lozada-Oliva, Katie Rejsek, Natasha Rao, Sahar Romani, Mimi Ton, Alisson Wood, Madeleine Mori, Charleen McClure, Chloe Blog, Janelle Tan, Elliott Sky Case, mal profeta, Raven Leilani, JinJin Xu, Kukuwa Ashun, Hílda Davis, dee(dee) Redd, Tiffany Troy, Malvika Jolly, Glynnis Eldridge, Aleece Reynaga, Ricardo Alberto Maldonado, Kiran Bath, Catherine Chen, Devin G. Kelly, Marwa Helal, Brionne Janae, Raymond Antrobus, I.S. Jones, Jess Rizkallah, Saeed Jones, Cortney Lamar Charleston, Silvina López Medin, Nadra Mabrouk, imogen xtian smith, and so many, many more. Forgive me that I can't list everyone.

To Toi Derricotte, Cornelius Eady, and my Cave Canem instructors Amber Flora Thomas, Evie Shockley, and Chris Abani. To my Cave Canem cohort who I wrote poems alongside that whole week. A special shoutout to Nicole Sealey and Dante Micheaux who taught me how to play spades during my week there.

To Tracie and Aryanna and our combined clumsiness and random injuries.

To Maurice Carlos Ruffin, Emilie Staat Strong, Kayla Min Andrews, and Annell López, who read through some of my last-minute revisions.

To all the musicians, muses, and historical figures that appear in the collection, I thank you for existing.

To Sarabande Books, thank you for believing in this book and publishing it.

To New York for housing me as a young poet.

To all former versions of myself: we did it. We planted loneliness and grew words. But we were never *really* alone. We had books. We had us.

To the New Orleans Public Library.

To anyone who's ever read my poetry when they could've been doing literally anything else with their wild and precious life. Dear readers, I thank you.

And finally, to New Orleans and all its existences: past, present, and future. I am made from you. May no water wash us away. I will forever remain faithful to you.

Karisma Price is a poet, screenwriter, and media artist. Her work has work that has appeared in *Poetry*, *Four Way Review*, *wildness*, *Adroit Journal*, and elsewhere. She is a Cave Canem Fellow, was a finalist for the 2019 Machester Poetry Prize, and was awarded the 2020 J. Howard and Barbara M. J. Wood Prize from the Poetry Foundation. She is from New Orleans, Louisiana, and holds an MFA in poetry from New York University where she was a Writers in the Public Schools Fellow. She is currently an assistant professor of poetry at Tulane University.

Sarabande Books is a nonprofit literary press located in Louisville, KY. Founded in 1994 to champion poetry, short fiction, and essay, we are committed to creating lasting editions that honor exceptional writing. For more information, please visit sarabandebooks.org.